WHITE-COLLAR MIGRANT WORKER

WORKER

MAKING YOUR WAY IN THE GIG ECONOMY

GERALD EVERETT JONES

LaPuerta
Books and Media
www.lapuerta.tv

———

Cover art by ximagination © 123RF.com
Frontmatter illustration by Gary Palmatier, Ideas to Images
Author photo by Lori Marple, Runkee Productions
Book design by La Puerta Productions, Santa Monica, CA 90405
USA www.lapuerta.tv

The case studies presented in this book are fiction.
Any resemblance to real persons is strictly coincidental.
NOTHING IN THIS BOOK SHOULD BE CONSTRUED AS LEGAL OR PROFESSIONAL ADVICE. PLEASE CONSULT A LICENSED PROFESSIONAL FOR QUESTIONS ABOUT LABOR RELATIONS OR EMPLOYMENT.

Direct reader and press inquiries to: bookstore@lapuerta.tv

WHITE-COLLAR MIGRANT WORKER

This little book is dedicated to you shapers of tomorrow,
who will find your missions in technologies yet to be
invented — possibly by yourselves!

YOUR NEXT JOB IS A PROJECT

HERE'S THE BAD NEWS: YOUR OLD JOB DOESN'T EXIST

YOU no longer have a job description. Duh, that's because you don't have a job. Instead, in your new incarnation as a white-collar migrant worker, you have an assignment. And associated with that assignment may be a task. But don't take those descriptions too seriously. You might find them misleading, needlessly confining, or totally useless.

> Job Description:
>
> --
> (Please write in disappearing ink.)

You don't have a position. You don't fit anywhere in the organization chart. That's because, in a legalistic sort of way, you don't work at any particular place. And under certain circumstances – for example, if things go south – it will be convenient for them to deny they ever even saw you.

You're not employed by the people who gave you the assignment but by a vendor that might call itself a *staffing agency* or a *consulting firm.* (There's a difference, which is unimportant for now.) Those people might not know you, either. They are filling a gap – usually on short notice. Something in your resume fit the client's spec. A screener in the staffing place couldn't find anything wrong with you. You might have even passed some kind of test. Don't let it go to your head.

Or, you're a known quantity to the consulting firm, but the client has never met you. And they gave you the assignment anyway.

You are a *temp,* which is a diminutive term often applied to casual clerical labor. But you could just as well be an expert database architect or literally a rocket scientist. You're still a temp. Your assignment has a specific start date and a projected end date. And end it will – count on that – sooner or later than anyone anticipates.

About the only element of this assignment that is set in stone is your labor rate. It might be hourly pay, a project fee, or a piece rate, but all the same, it's a done deal. There will be no promotions, no bonuses. And benefits? We'll defer that discussion, but suffice it to say, as far as perks are concerned, the only extra rewards you will get will be from your best friend in the mirror.

Overqualified!

Here's a piece of good news. You probably think you're overqualified. But that word has no meaning within the context of a temporary assignment. In the traditional world of permanent employees, *overqualified* describes employees who are likely to be unhappy because they are not sufficiently challenged, who may resent taking direction from less experienced team members, and who will probably start lobbying for a raise from day one. But since, in your new circumstances, the labor rate is fixed, and since you've already agreed to the terms of the assignment, neither you nor the client has anything to complain about. If you're overqualified, you're simply bringing more expertise to the assignment than they think they need.

But, beware: Use of the term *overqualified* with a contract employee can be code for:

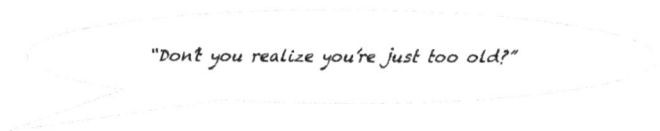

"Don't you realize you're just too old?"

Overqualified means you might be competition. Or you might dress old-school and not fit in with the after-work drinking crowd. No young middle manager wants to hire – much less listen to advice from – her mother.

From your standpoint, understand that being overqualified is your secret, mandatory qualification to succeed as a consultant. That's because you probably have enough experience and judgment to correctly analyze the client's business situation. And with your objectivity as an outsider, you may be uniquely qualified to find out exactly what's broken and needs fixing – not just the perceived problem your assignment was intended to solve.

Now, here's the biggest mistake you are likely to make: You will be eager to prove you are "just as good as" a so-called permanent employee. You want to prove that you deserve to be retained, as soon as your worth is recognized, as a direct hire with a real position, an eager staff, a corner office, and a handsome package of benefits.

?!

This "perm job" will not – indeed, <u>should not</u> – happen.
Don't <u>expect</u> to be hired. Don't even <u>want</u> it!

Yes, there are assignments billed as *temp-to-perm* or *contract-to-hire* – meaning, "We get to sniff you for a few months before we commit to doing it for real." However – and this is one of the main themes of this book – attractive as that prospect might be, the perm jobs are fast disappearing. That person sitting in the corner office who seems so comfy might already be dead and just not know it yet.

Your strategic advantage is that you will soon know how to survive – and thrive – as an independent contractor. And the freedom you will enjoy as a result of gaining that skillset will make you downright invincible in the workplace of the New Economy. (You could end up gifting the other guy a copy of this book.)

SHE WENT FROM CLERICAL SUPPORT TO PROJECT MANAGER IN THREE DAYS

CONSIDER THE CASE OF...

Yolanda O. Upshaw (Y.O.U.)

Until a few months ago, Yolie was a marketing manager in charge of an 18-person Web design team at a major advertising agency. But when the agency was acquired by a larger competitor in the U.K., the new owners decided to consolidate all online development efforts under the auspices of the London headquarters, with major chunks of the hands-on design and coding subcontracted to programmers in Mumbai. (Some of the U.K. folks lost their jobs, too.)

Fortunately for Yolie – and hugely significant for her future role as a consultant – the weekend after she got her last paycheck she was invited to her friend Megan's birthday party. We'll spare the irrelevant details, except that this all-girl event involved several pitchers of Margaritas at a local Mexican restaurant. After Yolie had had a few, she noticed that Lucinda, who was sitting directly across the table, was convulsed in giggles. Yolie thought this odd since the word was Lucinda had been out of work for more than a year, and it could be assumed she'd have trouble coming up with her fair share of the check.

"I heard you were semi-retired," Yolie said to Lucinda. With the benefit of alcohol, the question was more frank than might have been polite.

"It's true I take more vacations now," Lucinda replied with a grin. "When I'm not working."

"So you *are* working?"

"Oh, yeah. Mostly editing – e-zine articles, technical papers, books. Say, *you* could do that."

Yolie didn't realize until just then that it was already public knowledge she'd lost her job. And so Lucinda wrote the name of a staffing agency on the back of a napkin and shoved it across the table.

The result was Yolie's first assignment with the Aardvark Agency.

The application process was easy and much less complicated than Yolie expected. She completed a short form on Aardvark's website and attached a current resume. She also checked a box indicating she'd been referred by a colleague and provided Lucinda's name. Yolie received an automated email reply immediately, stating that her application had been received and a "talent agent" would be contacting her. She got the call the next morning. The agent invited her in for a screening interview before the week was out. The interview was brief, and the agent was mostly concerned about which labor categories Yolie felt suited for. "Website editor" was the standout, along with "copyeditor," "proofreader," "technical writer," and "advertising copywriter."

It was obvious to Yolie that the agency was not particularly interested in her managerial skills or experience. She agreed to a minimum acceptable hourly labor rate, which actually seemed a bit high compared to her former salary – until she realized she'd only be working part-time. She filled out some paperwork, including agreeing to submit to a background check and drug testing. She understood she would be a W2 employee of the agency, and she would be paid for overtime, if required, based on submission of an electronic timesheet. She also took a 15-minute test that showed she could use a word processor and catch spelling and grammar mistakes.

On the following Monday, the agent called to ask whether Yolie was available to work. (They'd done a cursory, online background check, and the client didn't require the drug test.) When she said yes, she was given instructions to report to Sturm & Drang Architects downtown at 8 a.m. on Tuesday morning. The agent said Yolie should be prepared to work long hours and that this short assignment would definitely be over by late Saturday night. When Yolie asked about the type of work, all the agent knew was that it fell under the category of copyeditor.

The next morning Yolie reported to the Sturm & Drang reception desk 10 minutes early. She signed the visitor's log and was given a stick-on badge with her printed name and the label ESCORT, which apparently meant an authorized person had to accompany her anywhere she went in the building. Promptly, a security guard appeared and led her down two floors into the Reprographics department.

The guard swiped his employee badge to open the steel door. The room was huge – maybe half the size of a football field. This end was covered with long, cafeteria-style tables. At the far end were two high-volume digital printers, each about as long as a semi-trailer truck.

The machines were quiet, and there was no one else in the room. Eight of the tables were covered with foot-high stacks of newly printed pages.

"Where is everybody?" Yolie asked.

"They worked late last night," the guard said. "Take a seat and Oswald will be down in a bit to give you instructions."

"Is it okay for me to look at the pages?"

He smiled. "Knock yourself out. But see it all stays in order."

After the guard had left and Yolie sat down, she

didn't start reading right away. She figured this guy would show up any minute and explain her task.

After 20 minutes when she was still alone, she couldn't help taking a look. Each stack had 11 copies of one section of a highly technical document. A section was about 10 pages. The pages were printed in color with diagrams and text, three-hole punched with the section copies separated by colored slip-sheets.

This was a bid document for a multimillion-dollar contract to remodel an airport terminal in Glasgow, Scotland. The sections were stacked in table-of-contents sequence, the stacks on one table comprising one or two volumes of the submission – although the Technical Proposal volume was so big it covered three tables. The other volumes were Executive Summary, Management Plan, Past Performance, Cost, Terms and Conditions, and Environmental Impact.

Still no Oswald, so Yolie started reading in earnest. With this huge, multi-volume document already printed, she couldn't imagine why they'd need a copyeditor. However, she did spot the occasional typo.

Why did they rush to print if there were errors?
Am I supposed to proof all these pages by Saturday –

<u>*all by myself?*</u>

A tall, twenty-something man came through the door. He was wearing a hoodie and jeans. His hair was a mess, and he hadn't shaved in days.

"Where's my section?" he demanded.

"Are you Oswald?"

"Oswald? No, I'm Tim."

"Okay, Tim. What's the title of your section?" Yolie remembered seeing a Table of Contents and found it.

"IT Infrastructure Upgrade Plan," Tim said.

"Let's see," Yolie said as she walked over to another table. "That would be in the Technical Proposal volume, Section 3.2.3."

"Quite right," he said, following right behind her. He found a chair and pulled it up to the table where his section was stacked.

"Would you be doing a final q. c.?" Yolie asked, worried that he'd see typos that presumably she should be catching.

The guy actually laughed. "No, I'm reading for the first time. My boss wrote it, and he's mostly clueless, but they had to have something, and I was on family leave."

"Weren't you able to review it online?"

"They were in a big, damn hurry. They're always in a hurry. Do you mind?"

So she resumed her seat and watched in amazement as Tim started reading. To her dismay, he was soon scrawling all over the sheets. He wasn't just adding commas and correcting spelling – he was crossing out entire paragraphs.

Tim was still working on his section when another engineer walked in – a middle-aged woman, not dressed much better and looking just as weary. She wasn't Oswald, either.

She wanted to review her section, which was "Temporary Logistics and Provisioning" in the Environmental Impacts volume.

Her name was Pom, and she, too, could not resist marking up her pages.

Finally, in came Oswald.

"What are they doing?" he asked Yolie in a hush.

"Reviewing their sections," she said. "And marking them up!"

"It's too late for that," he fumed.

"So should I tell them?"

"No, no," he said. "We're going to have to find a way to make those changes. There's a team of word processors upstairs. I'll take the pages up there, but I can't afford to spend any time down here. You'll have to coordinate."

"Didn't you want me doing copyediting?"

"That's just a labor category," Oswald said. "I'm the proposal manager. But do they listen to me? Obviously not. We printed everything so we'd have time to stuff the binders and do quality control. I needed you to eyeball the pages to make sure there are no smudges or streaks."

"But I couldn't help seeing – there are typos."

"Least of our worries," he said. "Obviously, these clowns have other ideas."

And he left the room abruptly, despite the fact that he'd told her he'd take the markups with him.

Her first day went to 9 p.m. by the time the last reviewer called it quits. By then there had been a dozen of them in there furiously marking up their sections. Not one of them saw fit to leave well-enough alone.

Early in the day, after she'd seen what Tim had done, Yolie found a yellow pad and decided she should keep a change log. She reasoned that if any section had more than five pages that needed correcting, the whole section would have to be reprinted. That's because printing and inserting change pages would be a cumbersome manual process. What's more, it could cost more labor hours if a later quality-control step found there were pages missing or inserted out of order. The five-page limit was purely a guess, but she felt she had to have a rule that applied to everyone.

When there were five or fewer marked up pages in a section, she replaced each removed page with a colored slip sheet that stuck out the side. A glance at the table would show which sections were in work. In her log, she recorded author, section number, page numbers needing correction, and date and time of submission to WP. Otherwise, she noted the entire section had to be sent upstairs.

Saturday night, she soon learned, was the hard dead-line. Eleven copies of each volume had to be boxed and loaded into the company jet for transport to the client in Scotland. As Oswald was to remark later, "Somehow it all gets in a box."

Over the next two days, which also ran to a late hour, the room filled up with subject-matter experts who were reviewing their sections.

As the word processing team updated each section, they sent the document file to print. And the presses were humming again. The operator would bring the reprints to Yolie, who busied herself with inserting change pages or replacing entire section stacks.

On Friday morning, they were still making changes, and new faces were still showing up.

One preoccupied fellow who was wearing a tie seemed particularly impatient. He turned to one of his colleagues and asked, "What's going on here?"

The colleague deferentially pointed to Yolie as she said, "I don't know who she is, but ask her. She's running the show."

And that, dear reader, was Yolanda O. Upshaw's first – but far from her last – gig as a bona fide consulting project manager.

STAFF AUGMENTATION VERSUS PROJECT MANAGEMENT

WHAT'S THE DIFF?

YOLANDA'S EXPERIENCE points up the fundamental difference between staff augmentation and project management. When she was brought in, she was a placement from a staffing agency. She was a lone temp there to perform a straightforward task. Although he specified her task initially as copyediting, the proposal manager's intention was to have her do quality-control checks on printed volumes. But, as it turned out, she coordinated and supervised an entire document-revision process.

Even though in this situation Yolanda eventually managed a project, her role was not actually project manager. The distinction comes down to accountability – not only hers personally but also the responsibility of the firm that placed her at the client. A temporary staffer is responsible only for her individual performance. She will typically be supervised by a manager who is to be found somewhere on the client's organization chart. Her workgroup could be a composite team of client staff and temps. But the overall accountability for the work product – the delivery of a finished proposal, in this case – rested with the internal manager at the client.

So, in a staff augmentation assignment, an agency provides labor – individuals whose work is directed and supervised by the client's internal managers. Those managers are responsible for both building their teams and delivering work products.

By contrast, a consulting firm performs a project management function when its responsibility is to deliver a specific result. The project manager is a consultant and typically builds a team of outsiders who then perform at or in coordination with the client company to complete a project.

WHO DOES IT WELL?

And herein lies another fact of migrant work you should appreciate:

Staffing agencies that undertake project management contracts typically fail in the attempt.

That's because their own internal management is organized only to focus on assessing individual performance. For example, they keep metrics on employee attendance and customer satisfaction versus requirements. But they don't have a history or expertise in tracking overall project budget and schedule – or compliance of the work product with the client's expectations. The staffing agency may have placed a project manager on the job – but that person is reporting metrics to the client, not necessarily to the agency. To complicate matters, the staffing agency generally will not retain a project manager as a member of its own management team after the client's project is finished. Consulting firms know that retaining such expertise adds to the depth of their knowledge base so that they will have the capability to win and perform successfully on subsequent contracts.

So, know who is hiring you and what they are likely to expect:

- Staffing agencies provide people who must deliver outstanding performance.
- Consulting firms provide teams that must deliver a satisfactory result.

REDEFINE YOUR MISSIONS AND THRIVE!

In this example situation, Yolanda ignored her labor-category job title, as well as her intended assignment description. On her own initiative, she also redefined her mission. In this case, perhaps doing so seems like a happy accident. But needing to continually redefine your mission is not only typical for a white-collar migrant worker – it's also one of the most valuable services you can provide any client.

PAPERWORK? WE HAVE THREE FLAVORS

W2, 1099, OR CORP-TO-CORP

RELATED to whether you will have individual-performance or project-management responsibilities is the basic question of how the staffing agency or consulting firm will engage you. In the United States, these three options not only represent differences in responsibilities but also legal status as employee, temp or consultant, or contracted vendor. Other jurisdictions are likely to have similar categories.

W2

Refers to the IRS reporting form showing wages earned, taxes withheld, and benefit deductions. Under this arrangement, you are a direct employee of the agency or consulting firm, whether you are full- or part-time. Your employer is responsible for complying with wage-and-hour laws and may provide some benefits, for which you may qualify after an accrued number of hours or duration of the assignment. W2 employees who work for staffing agencies are typically paid hourly and must make weekly or biweekly reports on timesheets.

1099

Refers to the lump-sum reporting form the agency or consulting firm sends the IRS at the end of each year. Taxes are not usually taken out unless the IRS requires backup withholding. Under this arrangement, you are an independent contractor. You are not an employee of either the agency or the client. You are a freelancer and may not be eligible for benefits from the agency. You may be paid hourly or by project milestone. You may account for your performance by timesheet or milestone report. You typically render invoices to the agency based on those reports.

CORP-TO-CORP

This type of arrangement may apply to consulting professionals who have incorporated their own businesses. You may choose to do this if you build project teams by employing subcontractors. Your contract may be through an agency or directly with the client organization. Your status in either case is as an arms-length vendor, much as if you were an office-supply store or a computer-repair depot. You may invoice the agency/client for hours or milestones, but your accountability is typically at the project level for results. A portion of project fees or completion bonuses may be contingent on whether you stay on schedule and on budget.

SO MAYBE KICK IT AROUND?

FOR GROUP DISCUSSIONS, RANTS, AND SELF-ASSESSMENT

HERE ARE some suggested discussion starters should you want to have a group-think about this stuff:

1. Does the term *permanent employment* strike you as a bit odd? Dated, perhaps? Oxymoronic?
2. Even if a staffing agency or consulting firm is issuing you paychecks, you are, in effect, self-employed. How might learning how to act more like an entrepreneur benefit anyone who is trying to build a career?

3. How might not having a place in the organization chart be an advantage for you?

4. When an organization calls in an outsider as a consultant, is something probably broken? If so, how likely is the client to know what that something is?

5. A consulting engagement typically ends when the assigned task is complete or when a contractual time limit is reached. Should you aspire to be brought on staff by the client organization at that point? Why or why not?

6. How would you react if you learned you'd been retained simply to take the blame for a project that is almost sure to fail?

7. Project managers speak of "lessons learned" and "best practices." What are those, and how does the portability of those ideas support the job of a consultant?

8. Does innovation always involve risk? In what ways is a consultant more likely to discover innovations?

9. Considering the pace of technological change, educators often say they must train students for jobs that haven't been invented yet. What skillsets should be taught?

10. If you're a consultant, curiosity can be a valuable trait. How can you use your

curiosity to find problems that need solving without alienating your clients?

Please send your questions and comments to bookstore@lapuerta.tv

Related Titles

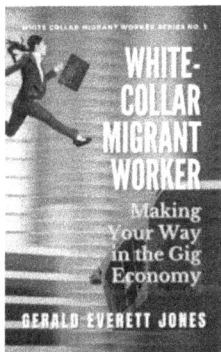

White-Collar Migrant Worker #1

Making Your Way in the Gig Economy

No job? Fresh out of school? Laid off? In the rapidly emerging gig economy, millions of workers will never have a job. But they can have a lifetime of profitable and satisfying assignments and projects. This handy little book will help you survive – and thrive – as an independent contractor. Don't wait for someone else to decide your future – here's how to write your own story.

Paperback or EBook

White-Collar Migrant Worker #2

11 Ways to Spot Fake News

Learn how to avoid misdirection on the information superhighway. Not to school hackers but to warn you, here are the most common ways someone can bend or break the truth to generate fake news. Many of these tricks rely on leveraging emotion to cloud logic. Another technique is to confuse cause and effect.

Paperback or EBook

White-Collar Migrant Worker #3

How Not to Abuse Metadata

No one need fear metadata or metadata analysis as long as it's summary-level data being shared. Unintentionally or deliberately using short-term trends or individual cases to generalize about the long term is a common pitfall.

Paperback or EBook

White-Collar Migrant Worker #4

Marooned! A Team Survival Game

In this team-building game, participants collaborate in small groups. A team score determines whether the team survives, and a private individual score helps participants evaluate their effect on the outcome.

Paperback (B&W) or
Kindle Print Replica (with color slides)

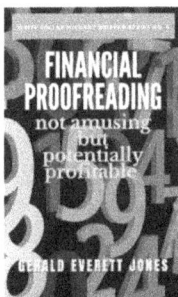

White-Collar Migrant Worker #5

Financial Proofreading: Not Amusing But Potentially Profitable

Learn how to make your financial reports both professional and classy. Diligent proofing in itself won't make a killer impression. But failing to proof for both accuracy and consistency could have woeful results. Perhaps numbers don't lie, but you can't afford a comma or a decimal point in the wrong place.

Paperback or EBook

White-Collar Migrant Worker #6

Technical Analysis Basics: Stock Market Charts

This coffee-break-short book will help you learn to spot trends in metrics applied to stock market price charts.

Learn the telltale characteristics of the Head and Shoulders chart pattern, along with how drawing its trend lines may forecast stock price highs and lows. Because Head and Shoulders can occur within short timeframes, it can be a useful tool for day traders and short sellers.

Paperback or Ebook

LaPuerta

www.lapuerta.tv **Santa Monica, California** bookstore@lapuerta.tv

The LaPuerta imprint and its logo – an open door – symbolize unlimited access to knowledge, opportunity, innovation, fascination, and delight.

Pitfalls of Business Reporting

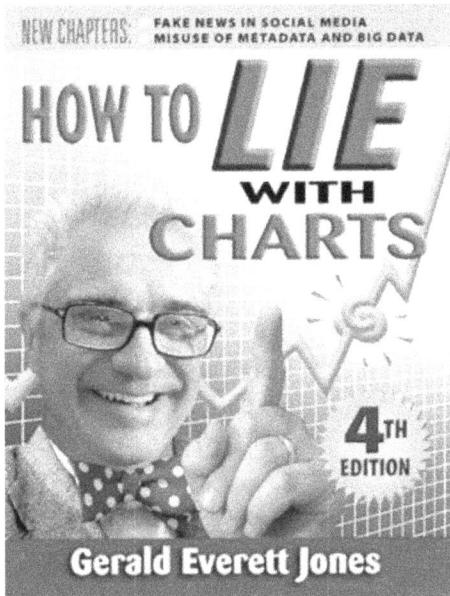

How to Lie with Charts – 4th Edition

Eric Hoffer award-winning textbook used in college-level courses in data visualization.

If you're using a computer to generate charts for meetings and reports, you don't have to be taught how to lie – you're already doing it. Focus is on the principles of persuasive – and undistorted – visual communication. It's about careful thinking and clear expression. *Don't blame the computers. People are running the show.*

Paperback or Kindle Print Replica

This humorous novel is also a case study in entrepreneurship
and the often zany world of consumer capitalism – inspired by a true story.

Mr. Ballpoint

Humorous Fiction (ages 14 and up)
Hardcover – Paperback – Kindle – EPUB - Audiobook

In 1945 Milton Reynolds introduced the ballpoint pen to the United States and triggered the biggest single-day shopping riot in history. Reynolds, an exuberant huckster who had already made and lost several fortunes, again became an overnight millionaire and then bragged that he "stole it fair and square."

Milton was a man ideally suited to his time—the post-war boom when the salesman was king and all of the rules had yet to be written. He was an old-fashioned, silver-tongued American peddler who would do almost anything—ethical or otherwise—to close a deal. His son Jim was a quiet honor student who couldn't tell a lie—even when he needed to.

Mr. Ballpoint is a father-son relationship story, told from Jim's point of view, about coping with Milton's outrageous schemes, then their sudden success. (It's a great Young Adult selection for book reports.)

"Forgotten history brought to life. If you ever wanted to know how to play the game of life and have a blast doing it, read *Mr. Ballpoint*. Perfect for our library and book clubs."

— **Deborah Vaden,** Manager of Libraries, City of Irving, Texas

"If only I had known about this marvelous invention before I started my writing career! No typewriter! No computer! The story calls to mind the old adage about pioneers and arrows. I salute Mr. Jones for his delightful and insightful tale."

— **Marvin J. Wolf,** author of *Rotten Apples: Tales of New York Crime and Mystery* and *For Whom The Shofar Blows*

ABOUT THE AUTHOR

Runkee Productions

Gerald Everett Jones has managed major proposal and business analysis projects in government, healthcare, and commercial sectors. He is the author of more than 25 business and technical books on digital media production, including numerous how-to books on applications such as Microsoft Excel and PowerPoint. He has hands-on background in IT systems development and was project leader on the ARTIS computer graphics system, a precursor of PowerPoint. He has often led seminars on the topic of achieving honesty and clarity in business presentations.

Gerald is also an award-winning novelist, and he is the host of the <u>GetPublished! Radio Show.</u> He writes the Thinking About Thinking blog on Substack geraldeverettjones.substack.com.

Reach out to him at geraldeverettjones.com and <u>book store@lapuerta.tv</u>

Gerald's Booklist

Fiction

Harry Harambee's Kenyan Sundowner: A Novel -
Multiple Awards
The Misadventures of Rollo Hemphill (#1 - 3): *My
Inflatable Friend, Rubber Babes, Farnsworth's Revenge
Mr. Ballpoint
Christmas Karma
Choke Hold: An Eli Wolff Thriller
Bonfire of the Vanderbilts / Bonfire of the Vanderbilts:
Scholar's Edition
Clifford's Spiral: A Novel* - Multiple Awards
Evan Wycliff Mysteries (#1 - 3): *Preacher Finds a
Corpse, Preacher Fakes a Miracle, Preacher Raises the
Dead* - Multiple Awards

Nonfiction

How to Lie with Charts - 2020 Eric Hoffer Award
Finalist in Business
The Death of Hypatia and the End of Fate
The Light in His Soul: Lessons from My Brother's Schizo-
phrenia (with Rebecca Schaper)
Searching for Jonah: Clues in Hebrew and Assyrian
History by Don E. Jones (Afterword)
White-Collar Migrant Worker (Series)

f 𝕏 ◎ a in g

www.ingramcontent.com/pod-product-compliance
Lightning Source LLC
Chambersburg PA
CBHW071742020426
42331CB00008B/2143